T0083668

Previously published

At the Gate
Perfect Disappearance
Mother Quiet

The Beds

The Beds

Martha Rhodes

Autumn House
Press

Pittsburgh

Copyright © 2012 by Martha Rhodes

All rights reserved. No part of this book may be reproduced in any form whatsoever without written permission from the copyright holders, except in the case of brief quotations in critical reviews or essays. For information, contact Autumn House, 87 1/2 Westwood Street, Pittsburgh, PA 15211.

"Autumn House" and "Autumn House Press" are registered trademarks owned by Autumn House Press, a nonprofit corporation whose mission is the publication and promotion of poetry and other fine literature.

Autumn House Press Staff

Editor-in-Chief and Founder: Michael Simms

Managing Editor: Adrienne Block

Co-Founder: Eva-Maria Simms

Community Outreach Director: Michael Wurster

Fiction Editors: Sharon Dilworth, John Fried

Associate Editors: Rebecca King

Media Consultant: Jan Beatty

Publishing Consultant: Peter Oresick

Tech Crew Chief: Michael Milberger

Intern: Caroline Tanski

ISBN: 978-1-932870-53-4

Library of Congress Control Number: 2011905783

All Autumn House books are printed on acid-free paper and meet the international standards of permanent books intended for purchase by libraries.

Autumn House Press receives state arts funding support through a grant from the Pennsylvania Council on the Arts, a state agency, through the Pennsylvania Partners in the Arts (PPA), its regional arts funding partnership. State government funding depends upon an annual appropriation by Pennsylvania's General Assembly and from the National Endowment for the Arts, a federal agency. PPA is administered in the Pittsburgh region by the Greater Pittsburgh Arts Council.

For Nancy B. Leverich and Judy Robbins for their early encouragement.
For Tricia Elam, my earliest writer friend.

Contents

I.

THE SMALL CANAL BETWEEN THEM

Into the small canal is Nothing

ever tossed? This is a dare-not-
venture-into place
and so persists, tannic and idle

for the rest of their lives.

IT FELL ON ME

It fell on me to write his stone,
purchased before I was born,
along with my mother's.
Easy to write hers. *Loving Mother of Me.*
But for him—what? beyond his name
and dates—four years since
the marble company asked me
for the words I wished inscribed.
It was never my ambition
to be the good daughter.
Was, though, to be

my husband's good wife.
And now, he's silent too—
and the western reaches of the bed,
his side, stay light, and a fault line
divides our small plot. What
to chisel into our marriage stone?
That he just regarded me as that
which he wished lived elsewhere?

Erasure. Dunes rising, and even
shorter days in the east.

COME TO ME, HIS BLOOD

Come to me, his blood,
so I may cup you,
be reservoir and ladle, both—
clean, store, and stir.
Then serve you back to him.

Come to me, his blood, ill,
so I may warm, sieve, and funnel
you back to him; his cheeks ruddy
again, his head in my lap.
The wind is up! and sails our boat

across Farm Pond, our friends
on shore waving us to picnic time—
a hammock-nap, a swim—
all four of us, all well.
Not dozens of summers ago,

but now, this final Sunday in July,
come to me, his blood. Don't rush
onto a lawn or street, don't seep—
but if you do leave him, if spilt,
you who cannot slow or thicken

redirect yourself—you must—come to me
and I will bring you back to him.

THROMBOSIS

A rat carried this week to us between its teeth and dropped
it at our feet and not even our youngest cat sniffed at it,
though the rat surely left his scent on each day, morning
through night. And the rat will find its way to us here, too,
where at the hospital I hold onto your foot lest you
be rolled away without me. We fear the rat will bring more
Weeks of Inability, both of us unable—though today I am
able to eat every doughnut New York City offers.

My grandfather was a baker from Vienna.

Perhaps he'd say to me today, *Doughnuts are in your blood.*

And what should I say about your blood, dear, not knowing
yet what's in your blood that brings us here this week.

When in the afternoon I cry, you sleep.
When in the morning, too, you slept.
You woke at noon then dressed then slept
To heal all day, all night, you sleep,
You sleep, you sleep, you sleep—
In the weeks beyond this, when fully healed,
You'll quit our bed at dawn; go to your field
And I'll reclaim our quilt. How long my sleeps?
You'll never know, nor should. Be well.

THAT NURSE

Who is she who washes you
where I would were she, hot sponge,
back in her pail closet, not lathering
over you while you, pink and drowsy,
forget the baths we've shared.

WHAT DO YOU PRAISE IN ME?

What do you praise in me?
Each night as sleep encircles,
my pink glow shelters you.
Do you, then, praise my smile,
scimitar I polish for you, beloved,
so that you may see morning, each,
as triumphant beginning?

I ask little but do ask this: Praise
murmured into my ear. You may, yes,

remind me my breasts are gentle;
my way with lamb roast sublime;
how for me the greenest wines sing.
And how light my soprano voice.
Friends of the highest orders
surround me, those master painters
of mountain swirls and sulfuric spouts

for it is my goodness attracts fineness
and I attract you, dear, and darling,
you praise me, do you not?

THE CONCUSSION

Let me remind you that the bile
his injury riled up arrived
on your pillow as you slept.

He would have forgotten
the shower's purpose
were you not there,
soaping him front and back,
your hair not clean yet, braided
and complicated to unbraid
when wet and foul;
the bed hastily stripped
then re-made by you
while he, propped in a chair
and snug in your robe,
stared at—
what—

For all of this, he still
may not be kind to you again—
concussions known to turn some rabid.
Your floppy retriever. Now he's weaving

toward coffee in the galley kitchen.
Retract your hand.

EVOLUTION

The golden and extraordinary frogs ate us
bug-less, then vanished somehow.
So, all over us this spring, mosquitoes,
returned, and triumphant, the low chorus
from the pond just memory, replaced
by a buzzing that sears through our ears
and bloodies—devours—our limbs and faces.
Carnage on our decks. We'll stay inside, mostly,

hereafter. What's happened to the frogs? Remember
when we *had* frogs? Do you suppose this is just another
extinction? What *are* frogs? the children sputter.
Our screens chewed through, we flee blanketed and hurtling
toward our car—but where go?—those animate engines
at our heels (in the rearview mirror, My God! what're *those*?)—

ANTICIPATION

She climbed the stairs
wanting to find them, and she did.
She climbed the stairs.
She knew they'd be there, two liars
at her table, plotting to rid
themselves of the one they wished was dead?
She climbed each stair.

NEXT MINUTE

I brought to him the cups of tea
he smashed across the room.
I brought to him the honey spoons
he pasted on the wall.

And brought to him the tissues
he wadded up his nose
and capsules quartered, and music
softened—

His fever barely weakened him—
he shoved our bed against the door—
who had we become, though I didn't care
just then—I pounded that door to hell.

Hell
was where I wanted him,
next minute not soon enough,
nor blink of eyes, nor breath.

THE PLEASURES AND INCONVENIENCES OF BEING DETESTED

Broken leg
Broken leg
And broken leg again.
And 81 stairs.
And no children so no visits from them.

Broken leg again?
Friends tired of all the errands and schlepping up those stairs.

How many times
Are you going to break That Leg? your doctor kindly asks.
And weren't they going to put an elevator in this building?
Weren't you going to move?

What is it with you and your bed, anyway?

SYLLABUS

Under my mother's death
I've found my own!
She schools me—quietly—
to forget Up There
so that I will not miss it.

I AM LOOKING AT HIS BACK AS HE EXITS THE SHOWER

To quietly touch that back, catching a drop
as it lets go his hair to course down his neck,
down between his shoulders. He'll spin around,
his drying off interrupted, to say, *What?*
The floor, ceiling, and wall of my heart
will then glaze over and explode. I close my eyes
to him. I don't want an ice chip to ever travel
my finger to my heart.

Every day now, tiles pop off the bathroom wall.
We could redirect the shower head, or just—
move, one or both, why not, out.
I claim Baker River as it opens in a rush.
A saddle of rock holds me.
The river's New Hampshire cold at first plunge,
then habitable, a gentle pound on my back.
I am looking at myself living there.

MISERY

That I've died, or because you've broken
your favorite wine glass, or lost your passport,
or because you yourself are ill—*why* you're miserable
won't matter to me—misery is what
I'll send your way: death will not sweeten me—
I will forgive only myself. Not you, not you.

Misery will fly toward you as you close
my eyes and pat my hair; as you
draw the sheets up over my head, a puff
of soot, my last gesture. Go, go. I will not
miss you though once I did—you'd left
our young bed to prepare lemonade.

You took so long.

WHERE TO

Before we have time to despise each other,
before it ages and causes aches so that I
swear at it, lie across it diagonally,
forego it for the sofa, I discard it,
infested,
the creatures finding entry and emerging
to feed on me as welts spontaneously
rise, entire pastures swelling,
14 weeks of sleeplessness, and ice chips
sliding down my slopes, and pills, baked salves,

the mud of me a wreck and every morning
I'm afraid of every cushion and wall, hotel,
train, afraid to leave home and to return.
And unwanted everywhere. Finally, out!
My beloved bed trucked away, tagged
so others will be sure to recoil—

but where dumped, where are things dumped—
and where will I end up and where, of course,
the underlying question, is he—

2.

TO THE SAILOR

50 foot seas.
30 foot boat.

5 foot 7 inch husband whose duffel I unpack,
whose orange squall jacket and whistle I now hold,

what sea held you so long?
Or who?

AFTER A LONG TIME OF NOT

the pink of his earlobes as he sleeps
is what she'd reach to touch.

Does he wish for something of her?

BANANA BOAT

I once sat on a stone wall built by my father
and looked across our green plush lawn, waiting
for my mother to come back to me by boat, sailing
forward through the swamp in back of our yard,
up onto our lawn, a boat filled with gifts for me,
filled with my mother, her arms outstretched,
my pretty mother would wade out into the rays
of our yard's private sun and run to me, up
the stone steps to where I sat squealing to be lifted
by her forever, lifted and adored for she had been
gone two weeks on a banana boat to Panama and so
the boat I waited for was yellow and filled with bananas
and I looked through the pines that bordered our yard,
into the swamp of frogs and snakes that froze over
in winter forming a fine skating pond—I looked
for the banana boat and would not come inside for lunch
but ate outside a sandwich and punch and stretched out
on the ledge and cried myself to sleep, my oldest sister
carrying me inside, stroking my whole body out of tantrum,
my beloved babysitter twirling my hair into banana curls
every day, until my mother arrived, by car, parked
in our circular drive, and opened the front door

and it was a lovely two weeks with the babysitter whom I loved
almost as much, wasn't it, and wasn't I taller now, and my hair
longer, and my skin brown from the sun, and more freckles,
and look—a banana necklace I would keep under my pillow
and worry with my fingers into tangled knots for decades
as I struggled to sleep each night, but couldn't, and can't now
because I wait and wait and wait and wait for his return.

AN IMMENSE

I liked sitting in our room
by the early morning window.
I'd watch him stretch his legs
just shy of violent cramp until
he'd wake, the bed's smell
an immense blend of sex so that
I'd rush back to him.
This blank room's smell
is like that, persistent, as I rest
against the wall; I'm merely
passing through, to visit
someone, though I am not
quite sure who, actually, and if
I am to say hello, or goodbye—

AFTER

After the *Now it's over,*
even the cutting boards split.
The recliner locks upright,
the ottoman refuses her legs,
the bathroom her spillage.
There is a chair, a rope, a beam.

But for the one who sits at his desk
humming, the day is gloriously lit.
How to stretch that light to her corner?
Or leave her corner? Or sing—
if only to show him she can, despite—
when her voice is a cracked tweet.

A friend urges, *Imagine a pitiless
and without dark place.* But for her,
the swim up river is easy. Familiar
the blind passage back to that moment
before, before he, who waited hungry
on that river's bank, pulled her out,

if not to devour her in the breathless open,
then to do what, and for how long,
and then, what after?

THE GATHERED

The river sludge hardens and cracks.
We pitch our tents in mile-long rows.
Branches, leaves, fox and deer tracks.
A few puddles pool, but there's little flow.

We're camped above, too tired to press
one more step; we sleep in fits—
the gnats, the howlings, the mess
of our lives bright in our eyes and lit

before us, our precious disasters.
This town's been claimed by the ridiculous—
by the should-have-known-betters
who assign us these lots, who welcome us

here as their own; we deserve this rot
and roll in it, thrive in it, and in turn
welcome those who follow us. *Need a bed?*
Rest here with us, friend. End of the line.

Dead end.

THE LAND PIRATES

The land pirates will come to grab my fields—
invade my cabinets, smelt my last gold.
For hidden cash they'll tap my walls.
No diamond chips. No pearls.

Un-ply the planks!
Then auction these nails!

Everything I own down the hill.
Everything I own sold to the town.

Out I'm put onto the gravel.
Out you go proclaims the gavel.
Out I go, and away.
All because I cannot pay.

SEX

Slow,
she hoped, when the porch light timer
shut off a minute after they entered
the house, dishes stacked on the counter,
sink full of pans they truly preferred
to delay until morning, humidity
evident on the walls and their hair.
Both of them smelled of butter,
corn, salad, and grilled steak. *Slow,*
she hoped, *but not lasting forever,*
not extended by restless bouts of sleep
interrupted easily by either's
slight shift of weight, or deep sigh,
to start up again. *Slow,* she reminded.
It burns—his half sleep heavy atop her,
their sweaty sheets tangled around her
middle, stickiness not drying between her
legs. But finally, night cooled down, the sheer
heaven of damp skin greeted by cool air.
Slow, but quick to finish, she hoped
that exceptionally humid evening, the last
dish wiped, as they headed upstairs—

how long they took, she doesn't now remember,
she wishes it took forever, as she confronts the other
burning that keeps her awake, not from desire,
or too much friction, but from the black acid
that bubbles in her mind and pours out her eyes
to turn them crimson, and down her cheeks
to form—was that, was that, was that
the last time?—two hot white rivers.

MY NEPHEW'S WEDDING

Into their wedding cake I dive. Into
their sweet futures, my face and arms.

Into their wedding cake my body entire.
Into their buttered roundness, I collapse.

INSTRUCTIONS FOR SOON, OR LATER

Do not say "Soon,"
or "Later," ever, please.
Instead, "Ten," or "Noon,"
or "After dusk, before dark,"
or "The last Monday in June,"
or "I'll be home for Christmas,"
or "For sunset on the dunes."

You, who hope to know me better,
know that for him, the one
I've finally finished waiting for,
I waited longer than I'll wait for you.
I'm sorry. Leave as you will—miss supper!
But if you plan return, state when,
or don't, and find these pillows with another.

STOLEN

I stole his field.
It's all mine now, flowers and grass.
I stole his field.
Dug it up to plant back home, (held
up the owner who gave me sass)—
but I persevered, bagged it fast.
I stole that field.

TRUE HOPE

That wet canine smell as you enter your new home.
Flies suggest: Avoid that room down the hall.
You're here with all you could bring—
your father's prayer shawl in its velvet pouch,
the Morris chair, Mission desk.

You navigate the rippled floors.
When lightning rings through the pipes
the kitchen brightens—a flash of true hope.
It is golden here for this demi-second. Bright.
You won't be frightened away.

3.

PLEASE DO NOT PERSIST

when I've told you that I do not go downtown.
Nor anymore out of state. No Cape, no
Mid Coast Maine at Christmas, my sister's
cottage empty of me. Not to the pharmacy—
no refills, no shampoo bought. Everything

delivered, the world—to me.

So last night when you and I drank up
the bar you're calling *Puffy's*, I confess
only this: I was here in bed, in this house,
alone—let me show you how I held myself
precisely at 9:45 until dawn, asleep.

So tell me, how there, then?

Last night, leave here? for Puf–fy's? No, mistaken.
Not I who kissed you, nor kiss you now! Nor ever will be.

WARNINGS FROM A FATHER

Since repotted it has turned against him.
Its purple wings shut when he nears.
Its lavender shoots hiss when he nears.
Let the plant dry up and rot.

The plant trips him any chance it gets
but don't move it or it will strangle *you*.
The plant lies to him and what it says,
I must promise not to repeat.

The plant I bestowed upon him?
Infectious and causes his kidneys
to fail. It's gotten into his safe
and stolen his gold. It's insinuated

itself into his Will. And now I, well,
get nothing—Less than the Warsaw Jews
I'll possess! Not even an overcoat. No boots.
No garage clicker. And no more husband for me!

Son of a bitch. Get rid of him. Run while you can.

PRIMAL

I'm scared of frogs.
No Bermuda for me, nor ponds.
I'm scared of frogs.
They're ugly. And creep up from bogs.
My nephew had one he called Jon.
I'd never make love on a lawn.
I'm scared of frogs.

TRANSFERRED

I've sold the field.
It's all theirs now, flowers and grass.
I've sold the field.
Deposited the money. Wild
to walk into a bank with cash.
Couldn't believe my sorry ass
could sell that field.

THE MEAL

She will eat it and then eat more.
She will wake to her skin turned
its color, and her hair, the whites
of her eyes, too. She will smell
of it. She will reek of it. She will
burst of it. So good it is.

The path between stove and chair.

The serving of it into her largest
bowl. The rich, brown reddishness,
the tawny spice of it. The spooning
of it into her mouth. The dripping
down her chin and neck, down
her cleavage.

(*Leave it there*, he'd say.)

Where he is, she does not know.
Even if he returns today

she will neither believe
nor disbelieve his explanation.
Perhaps he's husband and father
to countless others. Daughters. Ballet.

The endless runs for groceries. Fertilizer.

I like to walk. To Englewood! To Westport!
(He points to his worn out shoes and rock hard legs.)
Where he's been she does not know.
Weeks in fugue state out by Jones Beach?
Penniless weeks cruising the darknesses
under the George Washington Bridge?

Everywhere. Nowhere.

"Back in an hour. Shopping. We need stuff."
She tears up the note on the kitchen table,
its envelope overstuffed with tiny pink hearts
spilling into her lap, glittering between
the floor planks, hearts everywhere, unbroken.
Who is he who dared enter her sleeping?

Whose scent on her pillowcases this morning?

He, who would mistake the contents of her pot
for his own, who would eat his way to its bottom—
Let him chew the fat with his other brides.
Let him remain away! Such a headache now. Such
everything. Bad breakfast. Ruined lunch. Devastated dinner
he'll expect her to share. She wakes to a mouthful of husbands.

FOG HORN

The sheet's dark-on-dark pattern,
a flat dull sea, calm enough.

Something's floated to me,
content to warm itself

at my side. Familiar,
unsure if I'm asleep or not,

I nudge it away, not
to bruise or break,

but to assert. A small groan, then,
as it resettles, somewhere off—

I've begun my own noise—
of warning—a trembling at first,

then persistent, even confident,
through the night's steady fog.

THE RUBBLE

He lived against and through us, as a trickle
eroding a thick cloister wall. We weren't strong
though we were many. We saw the corn grow
just for him, our orchards ripen as he approached,
wither at his departures. Finally, depletion.
The great embarrassment of having given so much.

WHAT SHE'S DONE

He needed her
so he could work, and even sleep.
He needed her
and knew she'd stay, happily.
And she'd stay on for years to help
his dreams become. (Really, to keep
him needing her.)

MAY I?

What we say, when what we say is hurtful,
murders past kindnesses.

You are unlovable. You are unlovable.
You are unlovable.   To your grave with this you go.

But tonight, someone might like you. At least,
around your shoulders, he drapes the shawl that just silently
slipped to the floor, and presses your shoulders, lingers
in so doing and now sits across from you, *May I?*
and raises an invisible glass to toast your meeting.
You're a little high. You feel the blush. You must be
careful, though, this not quite real, *that* you know,
each second thrillingly, suspiciously, too long,
for instance, the splendor as he fixes his stare upon you,
as your face becomes an angel's, as chiseled, and as loved.

NEW BED

This, my new launch pad, from which my soul
may eventually, balloon-like, lift, its string
dangling from the ginkgo across the street while the rest
of me is en route to my family's welcoming plot in Sharon,
this bed may just represent my Grand Contribution after all,
curb-bound, its mites injecting my proteins into the poor
host for whom my body's mold will consent to conform.
So, here's to Good Sleep for that hapless finder of the up-for-grabs.

This small acreage I'll hold onto until my end occurs, with hope,
right on it, since timid I am to move this immaculate estate
just now—though I do hear the many offers to carry it anywhere
for me, and delicately, to boot, if not *preciously* one friend insists.
But can't he see, at hall's end, and dressed up frilly as you please,
my room, and in it, first purchase of my new life—

THE JADE PLANT

I want to go to the room
where the jade plant thrives

on the white pine floor. I want
to sit next to the plant all day

against the white plaster wall.
I want the room available all days

and evenings, it just one of the several
in my house arranged by me

for peaceful times. I want to go
to the room now though it does not exist

in my life yet. It is several hundred miles away
in a small town cottage by the river.

A friend who knows me best might say,
I can see you in this house with its contained yard.

I sit in the white room often. The plant
is old and thick. Its leaves are shiny deep green.

My sister arrives soon from Maine
and I'll give her this room for the week,

the jade, actually, our mother's—
what she last bought the eve she lost

all memory of what it is to buy something,
to recognize what it is you want, to point

to it and say, *That should be mine now.*
And then it is.

Acknowledgments

Love and gratitude to Lynn Emanuel, Kate Knapp Johnson, Howard Levy, Daniel Tobin, Ellen Bryant Voigt, and C. Dale Young for their responses to poems in manuscript. Thanks, too, to Bridget Bell.

The two frog poems are for Cleopatra Mathis. *Banana Boat* is for Jeffrey Harrison. The "Puffy's" poem goes to none other than Ryan "Omarahu" Murphy.

And finally, infinite gratitude to Michael Simms and Autumn House Press at large.

Poems from this manuscript appeared in:
Agni; *Cerise Press*; *Connotation Press: An Online Artifact*; *Laurel Review*; *Massachusetts Review*; *New England Review*; *Pleiades*; *It's Not You, It's Me*; *Salamander*; *Women's Studies Quarterly*; and *Zone3*.

Martha Rhodes is the author of three previous collections of poetry: *At the Gate, Perfect Disappearance,* and *Mother Quiet.* She teaches at Sarah Lawrence College and the MFA Program for Writers at Warren Wilson College. Rhodes is a founding editor and the director of Four Way Books in New York City.

The Autumn House Poetry Series
Michael Simms, General Editor

OneOnOne Jack Myers
Snow White Horses Ed Ochester
The Leaving Sue Ellen Thompson
Dirt Jo McDougall
Fire in the Orchard Gary Margolis
Just Once, New and Previous Poems Samuel Hazo
The White Calf Kicks Deborah Slicer • 2003, selected by
        Naomi Shihab Nye
The Divine Salt Peter Blair
The Dark Takes Aim Julie Suk
Satisfied with Havoc Jo McDougall
Half Lives Richard Jackson
Not God After All Gerald Stern
Dear Good Naked Morning Ruth L. Schwartz • 2004, selected by
        Alicia Ostriker
A Flight to Elsewhere Samuel Hazo
Collected Poems Patricia Dobler
The Autumn House Anthology of Contemporary American Poetry
        Sue Ellen Thompson, ed.
Déjà Vu Diner Leonard Gontarek
lucky wreck Ada Limón • 2005, selected by Jean Valentine
The Golden Hour Sue Ellen Thompson
Woman in the Painting Andrea Hollander Budy
Joyful Noise: An Anthology of American Spiritual Poetry Robert Strong, ed.
No Sweeter Fat Nancy Pagh • 2006, selected by Tim Seibles
Unreconstructed: Poems Selected and New Ed Ochester
Rabbis of the Air Philip Terman
The River Is Rising Patricia Jabbeh Wesley
Let It Be a Dark Roux Sheryl St. Germain
Dixmont Rick Campbell
The Dark Opens Miriam Levine • 2007, selected by Mark Doty

The Song of the Horse Samuel Hazo

My Life as a Doll Elizabeth Kirschner

She Heads into the Wilderness Anne Marie Macari

When She Named Fire: An Anthology of Contemporary Poetry by American Women
Andrea Hollander Budy, ed.

67 Mogul Miniatures Raza Ali Hasan

House Where a Woman Lori Wilson

A Theory of Everything Mary Crockett Hill • 2008, selected by
Naomi Shihab Nye

What the Heart Can Bear Robert Gibb

The Working Poet: 75 Writing Exercises and a Poetry Anthology Scott Minar, ed.

Blood Honey Chana Bloch

The White Museum George Bilgere

The Gift That Arrives Broken Jacqueline Berger • 2009, selected by
Alicia Ostriker

Farang Peter Blair

Shake It and It Snows Gailmarie Pahmeier

The Ghetto Exorcist James Tyner

Where the Road Turns Patricia Jabbeh Wesley

Crossing Laurel Run Maxwell King

Coda Marilyn Donnelly

Shelter Gigi Marks

The Autumn House Anthology of Contemporary American Poetry, 2nd ed.
Michael Simms. ed.

To Make It Right Corrinne Clegg Hales • 2010, selected by
Claudia Emerson

The Torah Garden Philip Terman

The Beds Martha Rhodes

• Winner of the annual Autumn House Poetry Prize